Attempting flight

Upside-down without a net

The art and words of Kristen Jongen

Soul Soup Publishing, LLC, Traverse City, MI

Published by Soul Soup Publishing, LLC, 109 S Union Street, Suite 202, Traverse City MI 49684
Design and layout by Robin Appleford 6661 Mathison Rd S, Traverse City, MI 49686

ISBN: 978-0-9773862-1-5
Printed in Hong Kong

Many thanks

Thank you to my children: Anya, Mia and Van. You are my glue.

While I only get to borrow you for a while before you grow to fulfill your own destiny, being your mother has been the greatest privilege of my life.

Mom, Dad, Talisa, Katie, Todd, Janet, Tina, Heather, Tony, Robin — you held onto me when I was slipping away. Thank you for the life ring. I hold my tribe dearly. I love you.

Thank you, to all who have supported my work with such vigor. Your emails and letters mean more to me than you will ever know.

Thank you to Robin Appleford, my layout artist and friend, for once again taking my words and art and creating something visually stunning. You make this paper world go 'round.

Thank you, Kathryn Hack, for your steady confidence and for editing my words in a way that is true to my voice. Your wisdom and candor encourage me when I am frightened. Your mentoring has held my virtual hand for years.

Thank you to every relationship that has bent me in different directions, ruffled my feathers, plucked my nerves and steadily healed my heart *(yes you, James)*. You put me to the test, and faithfully remind that love is bigger. Thank you to my steady tribe of old and new. I love you.

4

This book is dedicated to my old friend Babe.

Babe was a Black Lab / German Shepard mix.

She died in the spring of '08 at age thirteen.

She healed me in many broken places.

contents

"When Is The New Book Coming Out??"

How many of my anxiety-filled dreams have started with that question!

"Wasn't it due last year?"

As the final chapters of Attempting Flight are being assembled into a contiguous whole, I'm extremely grateful I've come this far. The book is three long years behind schedule, but not because I haven't been writing. I have filled journal upon journal. It is not because I don't have fresh artwork to accompany the stories. I may have more paintings than I can use. It isn't because the last five years have not been pumped with lesson after lesson on love, letting go, more letting go, mercy and rebirth.

No.

today I
stop

I breathe
deep and rest

with grateful
tears
I
weep

because
I have
come
so far

The mental block in finishing this new book is not due to lack of material. Monumental changes moved me slow and steady toward what I hoped would be a positive account of my own metamorphosis.

The block that kept me most apprehensive was, "How can I creatively pull together a string of mishaps into a tidy, inspirational feel-good? How do I duplicate a sense of wonder, when my innocence is gone?

While writing my first book, Growing Wings, everything was fresh and new. Even my grief was green. My wounds were so open I was busy plugging leaks. It is another stage in the metamorphosis, when the outer shell hardens to protect a fragile interior.

But what happens when the wounds start to heal— when fresh blood is pumped from a mending heart? I wish I could write that, upon the close of Growing Wings, I sailed away with my new man into the blissful, uncomplicated life I thought I deserved. I wish I could report losing ten pounds without even trying and, when not distracted by sexual rhapsody, I devised educational-culinary games for my children and me to play (while learning French).

I wish I could say it has been easy.

the transformation
from crawling to walking
is awkward

at best.

The thought of flying
Seems light years
away.

During many of those months I was black-cloud angry. How can I write an inspirational

book when I'm afraid of the jaded thoughts filling every crevice in my mind? How do

I expose gut-wrenching rage without soliciting a, "What happened to her?" response

from my readers? How can I write confidently about flight, while fearing I might

remain in pieces on the ground?

I will tell you.

I keep on writing, and praying that as long as one foot moves in front of the other

a light will appear that is bright enough to navigate me through the day.

I've come to accept the fact that adult adolescence is just as awkward as the acne and

zits, insecurity and goofiness, unsure footing and lanky arms that plagued my teens.

Now my adult butterfly has had that same, unwelcome pause between the shedding

of its cocoon and the discovery of her wings.

There were days and nights when she hung upside down to let her wings dry. It took time to evaluate her new shape, regroup and release the past in order to claim the present. Healing takes time.

If you're at a point in your life where you're moving into your next unfathomable phase, I hope that (while gripping on for dear life) you might recognize yourself in my own journey. I pray as you gain strength, confidence and a new perspective you'll embrace a rowdy sense of humor... while you dangle upside-down without a net.

Mostly I pray you won't get too comfortable. Attempting flight requires a conscious effort.

As your beautiful wings dry, never turn your spirit from your dreams.

never forget
who you are

Love
is
bigger

You have always been a winged creature.

You are not merely resting...

You are preparing to fly!

As always, remember you're not alone. We are brothers and sisters in this exhilarating, fascinating,

formidable journey called life.

Come fly with me!

your friend,
kristen

attempting flight
was Laden in duality...
an inate desire that Felt
akwardly like leaving the flock

Until the others
discovered
their
wings also

after witnessing
that one
of them
Could Fly

Attempting flight

I'm going through an awkward transition in my life. A place where nothing seems to fit. The life behind me seems small, and the one in front feels large and impossible to fill. Like an adolescent teenage boy, lanky limbs and giant feet stumble beneath me. I have outgrown tired roles and am clumsily trying to define my new ones.

A butterfly - me? Ha!
I feel like
an obtuse worm
with two wet feathers
... aerodynamically
impossible.

I'm a spectacle as I try to find my place. I feel conspicuous as I wobble around. Lacking confidence, I have no

idea if I'm even a candidate for flying.

As I hop clumsily from branch to branch, I spend equal time looking down at my past and shyly glancing up

toward my future. I see caterpillars at ease on the branch below and butterflies exulting in the air above. I

am neither. As this lumpy, wet, eager-to-fly worm girl I try to balance myself, sure of only one thing. I can no

longer dwell on the ground. The urge to take flight, to evolve is overwhelming.

I've prayed to become the person God wants me be. In tear-soaked desperation, I've heard the call that says, "Yes, you can fly!" but in my haste, I missed the instructions — the part where God mentions I'd be doing the grunt work. He didn't turn on the flashing neon sign that said I'd be giving birth to myself.

I thought enlightenment would sweep gracefully onto shore to beckon me aboard its sun soaked cruise. Squirming on the ground in agony was simply not in the mental picture.

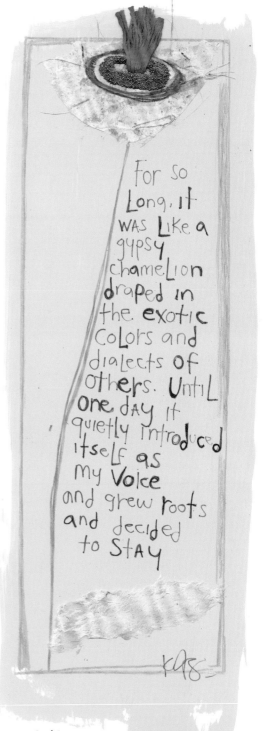

For so Long, it was Like a gypsy chameLion draped in the exotic coLors and dialects of others. UntiL one day it quietly introduced itself as my Voice and grew roots and decided to stay

KGS

After everything I've been through,

am I still
that delusional?

Taking flight is like being in labor; with every frantic inhale and exhale, the question arises whether or not it's worth it.

Should I shrink back into the life I had before or adopt the complicated winged-suit and believe someday it will fit

me? Is it worth the pain?

I want to live a maximum life, a life of actualized potential. I want to be limitless. How do I do this?

The answer I've heard, and heard again is to practice saying, "yes."

When I'm challenged to fly in a new direction, I will consciously try on *yes*. And not look down.

I wont die with my song inside me. I sing everyday my eclectic tune-arms wide raw heart exposed. I laugh as I make up words knowing I will and perservate find my way song is reduced when my sweet in moments of to a raspy whisper despair...but I sing Still I Sing, Sing Sing my song will not be caged my radiant eyes will give it away my song has broad flowing wings that effortlessly Soar, and fill the sky with wild Colored Sprinkles of me

kristen gog

It is an effort but I've started. I've dared to un-stick the creaky window and let in some fresh air. I thought that would be the hard part but it gets worse. As I say yes to each new dream, I'm still the gangly teen who doesn't fit in.

I didn't realize that in harnessing my potential I would appear the eccentric artist sitting gawkily in a pilots' lounge full of testosterone-bearing males; or the lone peace activist making her unsteady voice heard in city commission chambers. I didn't realize I'd feel inept and out of place and even a fool at times — as I try on my new suit of wings.

In my mind's eye, I thought I would be welcomed into my fabulous, new life with open arms. The truth is, there is an energy that can limit our reach.

Our own ego the ultimate naysayer of our fate.

We think to ourselves, "When I climb out onto that ledge, there will be people who'll watch amused, and gladly wait for me to fall."

Making the decision to climb out there and fly is hard enough; holding the space for myself can be brutal!

Being the bumbling girl in a room full of raised eyebrows is nothing short of terrifying. "Ground school,"

as they call it in flight training, materializes for me as a reality that has cracked my brain wide open. It's

rocket science. I'm learning things I would never have dreamed possible back there, squirming on the

ground. At the same time, I am shocked and blindsided and furious at the difficulty! Like a toddler trying

to stand, I have permanently skinned knees. But I can't go back. I have seen the possibilities and felt the

exhilaration of my first take off!

What A fabulous view of the world it is from the air!

Having flown through my own limitations,

it is impossible to ever-again live

contentedly on the ground.

"It is not only fine feathers that make fine birds."

–Aesop

Journal, May 30, 2005

Going Home

I slept in my parents' bed last night. I've taken to spending the night at their home on random occasions. Driving a mere 10 miles from my own house, I feel like I'm going on vacation, or rather, "going home" for a few days.

I lived with my parents for six months after I split from my husband. My son was born while living here.

Since that time, I've been getting steady on my single-Mom's legs. I moved into a home in the woods, near the big bay. My folks live on an intimate inland lake; two different synergies. It is a beautiful sunny morning, and a

we blindly travel Various paths on Numerous Journeys... searching for a Singular destination ...and yet Our illuminated souls have always contained The Light that will Lead US home

water skier is smoothly whipping by, led by the hum of a boat motor.

My parents are gone, visiting my sister. There is a soothing comfort in being here.

The lake is still and serene. The sun is bright at 7:30 a.m. I sit here feeling very

much at peace, wearing my Moms slippers and sweat pants and drinking coffee

from one of their mugs.

I didn't grow up in this house; they've lived here only seven years. I'm not familiar

with this side of town. Maybe it's the energy of my parents radiating from this

place that is relaxing, or perhaps the familiar scents and sounds that provide

comfort. My kids relax and think they are on vacation too. It has been a jagged

year for all of us.

All my "to-do" projects are on hold while we're here. I'm able to read without

compulsively jumping up to clean something, change a light bulb or repair any of

the million things going wrong with my own home. I bark at the kids less. They're

free to explore the pond across the street (they caught a fish yesterday), practice

gymnastics on the beach and make forts out of beach towels and chairs. Oh, and

the love of all loves – to watch the Disney channel (we have no TV at home). This

place is paradise to them!

have faith
breathe peace
know mercy

Old prom dresses hang in the closet downstairs and the girls have a hay-day digging through remnants of my childhood. Old yearbooks, love letters and silly photos are an endless source of curiosity and amusement. All too soon they will have prom dresses and love letters of their own.

Maybe it's the way my Mom decorates that makes this home so inviting. Or could it just be the casual atmosphere? Maybe the sense of protection my parents offer makes me feel safe. I get to feel like the "daughter" again, taking reprieve from the crazed, often-confused and harried single mother, business woman, artist, lover and home owner; a heavy shell that can weigh me down so easily.

I am blessed to have parents who are endlessly generous, and a place where I can find shelter, take off my armor, and rest.

29

Please don't leave

My three year old son has the looks of a sun-kissed surfer and the soul of a Teamster. His blond locks curl at the ends near his shoulders and he is blessed with giant, beautiful blue eyes. He loves to play in the sand, and says, "Hey, Dude!" when inspired.

This little guy has kept his sisters and me on our toes since the day he was born. He came out of the womb making car sounds. He loves wheels and motors and is so tough even his pre-school teachers shake their heads.

His favorite things are big trucks and loud motors. When he was two, he took apart his former high chair with a screwdriver. When I came over to see what he was up to he said, "No Mama, this dwane dwus," meaning, "Back off woman, this is man's work. It is dangerous."

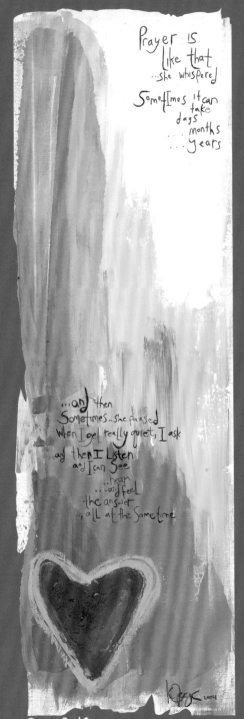

Prayer is
like that
...she whispered
Sometimes it can
take
days
...months
...years

...and then
Sometimes..she paused
When I get really quiet, I ask
and then I Listen
and I can See
...hear
...and feel
the answer
all at the same time

His favorite phrases are, "Cause I said so," and, "I don't like him," to

anyone who may look sketchy. Fear is not in his vocabulary.

Since his third birthday, my son has become increasingly upset as a

toddler's version of separation anxiety has set in. He breaks down in tears

if I leave the room or if I don't wait for him to come with me. Through

impending panic, he gasps, "Mama, pweeze don't weave me." It always

stops me in my tracks.

Gone is the meat-head who loves dirt under his fingernails. What remains

is a tiny, vulnerable little boy who is afraid of being abandoned. He cries

monsoon-quantity tears when I leave his side. I cradle his little cheeks.

"I will never leave you," I reassure him every time, no matter how rushed

or frazzled I feel. This phrase produces a visceral reaction for me as much

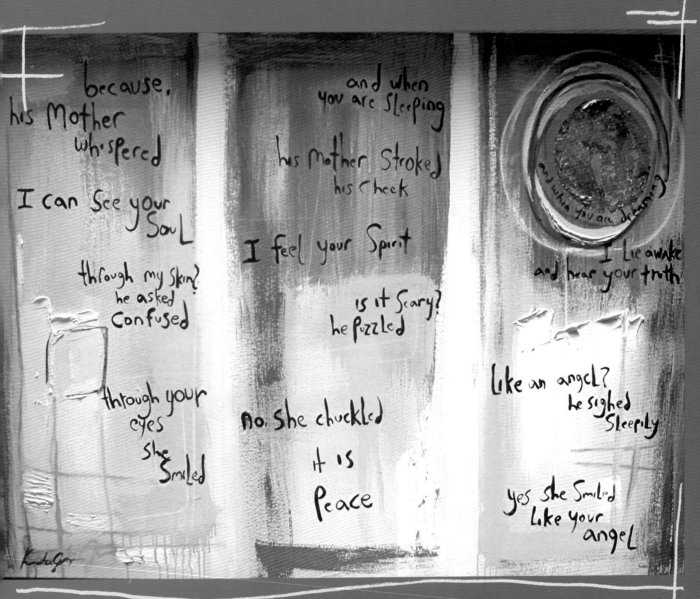

because,
his Mother
    whispered

I can see your
        soul

    through my skin?
    he asked
    confused

    through your
    eyes
        she
        smiled

and when
you are sleeping

his Mother stroked
    his cheek

I feel your Spirit

        is it scary?
        he puzzled

No. She chuckled

    it is
    Peace

and when you are dreaming

            I lie awake
and hear your truth

Like an angel?
        he sighed
        Sleepily

yes she Smiled
Like your
        angel

Close your eyes and know that on this journey of this world in this skin right here right now 'I am here' and you are not alone

as the fear does in him. It pulls on a deep heartstring.

The little boy in him speaks to the little girl in me: the little girl who recognizes the depth of his terror; the little girl who is also terrified of being left.

As much work as I have done in therapy – journaling, spiritual seeking and soul work – there is still a powerful fear that resides in my gut much of the time. I wish it didn't materialize in something so needy and grossly un-cool as a fear of abandonment. I am trying to grow a new skin and with it comes waves of, "Come Here! Go away!"

When I bottom out emotionally, I push my friends away with a violent thrust, much like a dog shaking the life out of a rabbit between its jaws.

I get all twisted up as I try to spread these new wings and figure out who I am. I have done this by first figuring out who I am not. Every cement-laden step requires a huge effort. I concentrate tirelessly on moving forward

in order to avoid the landslide that sweeps me back to my past. I look behind myself a dozen times. I move forward painfully slow, all the while beseeching my safety net, my steady tribe, "I have to try this, so please, don't leave me." I say good-bye to love relationships in much the same way. I thrash about and push people away with vicious force. I am heartbroken when my own machinations work. I want to beg, "Please don't leave."

The truth is, people leave. Friends come and go. People die. Lovers can move on. The world is an organic place of movement. Even when people promise they will "never leave me," I cannot believe them. Things happen, and no one can truly promise they will be here from day to day.

the answer
to the chaos
became a
quiet holy
mantra

be still
be still
be still
be still
be still

The irony is, I am the one in motion. I am the person taking measures to leave. I am always moving away,

pushing off and kicking ferociously. Yet I am terrified of being left. Talk about a conundrum!

Of my own choosing I maintain a tornado of a life. I hold a fear that, as I rebuild one radical step at a time,

my tribe will eventually tire of my turbulence and zip up the teepee for good. The fact that they stay confounds

me. Miracles happen.

All the while the little girl in me holds tight to her fears of abandonment. It is real. It is a black- jagged stone,

gripped within her tiny hand.

When I get very quiet, I can talk to her. I hear that her fear is real. My little girl is less afraid of others

than of a much more powerful source... *me*. As I flail around like a fish on the shore, she fears the truth;

that I will once again... abandon myself and *us*.

So, as I care for my son, the solution seems to be this: be the same kind of mother to myself as I

would be for him. "I will never leave you," needs to come first.

I take a deep breath and repeat the mantra ... slowly, gently and with compassion.

"you are safe"

I remind myself. "I love you and I will never leave you." As the tension melts, she and I begin to relax.

Like the ebb and flow of the tides, people move

in and out of my life. I am no good to them as an

empty, abandoned shell. So long as I am alive, I

must commit to be there for myself first.

don't despair
she whispered

as she pressed a
small seed in
the palm of
my hand

..feel the subtle
rumbling under
your heels

and hear the
lyrics in the air
...have faith
in each other
she winked

and I felt
the same
sprout of hope
growing in
me

that is
healing
the
world

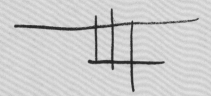

Maybe this is how God works. He starts in my own heart, healing my own soul, using my own voice, simultaneously reminding me that not leaving myself is the same as not leaving Him. And He will never leave me, because I am of Him. Our breath is the same and we are one.

I suspect this is the only real truth

He's a Fox

I am attempting to overcome my fear of attractive men

I will ignore the fact that my esophagus closes up and I can't breathe whenever one is near.

I will practice looking all men in the eye. If he happens to be attractive, I will continue as if he is not. I will

squash the voice that tells me I will look old and desperate when I am merely being friendly.

A case in point: there was a gorgeous man standing in a fast food line at an airport. His appearance stood

out from the crowd. Although I was a few people back in line, I couldn't stop staring at him. I rarely see guys

like this. He was tall and tanned, with a square jaw. He picked up his combo meal and walked away. I got my food and went to buy some gossip magazines at the bookstore.

I eventually meandered to my gate and there he was! He was headed to

Asheville, NC – same as me! He was stunning. I stared from behind my

US Weekly magazine. Of course, I never met his eyes, or even tried; I just

snuck looks from afar.

He boarded early, so I was sure he was seated in first class. I finished my mag and boarded

late, keeping my eyes peeled for a final look at him as I squeezed myself through the packed

747. His handsome face appeared in the back of the crowded aircraft. I looked at my ticket and

absolutely freaked out when I realized that my seat was the empty one next to his! My heart

started to pound. I began to sweat, with hyper-ventilating right around the corner.

My eyes darted around the cabin, and I quickly spotted the only other available seat. In sheer panic,

I grabbed it. I completely bailed out.

My Personal George clooney Sat by himself for three hours

because I was too self-conscious

to act normal and take my assigned seat. I was sure I would reek of insecurity, desperation and awe.

I told my friend Heather and she thought I was insane. She promised to help me. She looks like Pam

Anderson and doesn't appear to be afraid of any man. She is the perfect man mentor.

I practiced on a coworker's boyfriend. He is super-duper sexy, and while she was

introducing us I worked up the courage to look him in the eye. I relaxed because

he was taken and there was no pressure. We chatted for a few minutes, and I

couldn't believe he was a nice guy – and he was nice to *me*.

Hmm... so, overty attractive men can be nice, too? This requires investigation.

I'd written off this small but mighty segment of the male population because

they scare me.

My confidence obviously needs work. I am not afraid if they speak to me

first; just nervous if I'm forced to acknowledge some handsome devil, start

a conversation, or simply initiate eye contact. My friends and family cannot

believe I'm this ridiculous.

I practiced again with a client and her gorgeous husband. I thought it would be rude to look only at her, so I forcibly looked at him, too. I gave them both eye-contact, even though he made me queasy. "It's just business," I told myself. "This is not a bar. It is appropriate to look at him as well as her. She doesn't think you are after him, and he doesn't think you look desperate. They are here because they want to buy something. Snap out of it!" I felt like throwing up.

Three months later:

Oohh, I'm still working on it. I hadn't been successful yet, so I thought I'd give it another go. I picked the wrong venue to try out my new plan.

There is a yacht moored in the marina where I walk Darma every day – and a cute guy who is always washing it. He said "Hi" yesterday.

today I will attempt eye contact and give him a midwestern, How·do!

Later that day:

Umm, not a good idea. Two cute guys were washing the massive beast when I walked by. I said,

"Hi" – then quickly asked where the boat was from. Apparently, the staff on these vessels is

taught to keep tight-lipped. With a gorgeous Australian accent, the dark, curly haired one said,

"I am not at liberty to say."

Oops. I tried to cover for myself. "I mean, are you from Charleston?" (A yacht from Charleston

frequents our harbor) "Don't you guys come every year?" I tried to make it light.

"No." He said simply.

I looked like a scheming weasel.

"The boss is from New York City. He is a pretty high profile guy." He turned his back to continue

working, and it fizzled from there. I felt like an idiot.

"Oh, well, enjoy your stay," I said with a red face.

Oh my God. I wanted to crawl under a rock. You win some, you lose some.

But I will rally on. I will get over my fear. I may not end up in deep conversation with a Brad Pitt

look-alike (that's fine, though). It is not even about desiring a man who looks like that. It is

about overcoming a ridiculous insecurity. It is about feeling confident and worthy enough to

talk to anyone.

I will not be afraid to talk to my Abercrombie-model, Prince Charming, Brad Pitt look-alike or

any other handsome man with confidence – if and when he should come my way.

Stay tuned.

Say... Something real and I
will listen. My patience for
nothingness is all but gone. My
soul is dehydrated and Im surrounded
by white sugar. I lack
interest in humpity
Humps or lady
Lumps. Bend my
mind. Pt a kink in
my wha. Risk being
heard an I will
Celebrate with a
Universe based in Courage.
Say some- thing real
and my color will
return.

Spend your thoughts / like holy
currency... and I will invest in you too

creating what you defend against.

"You create the very thing, you defend against," says *A Course in Miracles*.

I finally get it this time.

After an impressionable first date with a man who has fascinated me for months, I suddenly make a clear

observation. Just as things were getting cozy, I pushed him away.

I profess I want an authentic relationship. "I want something real!" is my lament to friends. I'm tired of dating; exhausted by the constant fretting and fear. I am lonely, yet to observe my behavior from a distance, one would never get that impression. I'm the quintessential party girl.

Sifting through my bizarre dating behavior, I observe the barricade is thick and the filters are stringent. The only men I allow into to my life (through layers of skepticism) have one important thing in common: they are in one way, shape or form unavailable.

There could be identical twins standing next to each other; one is eager and attentive. There is no question about his intentions. This remarkable, rare bird goes overboard with his thoughts, words and actions.

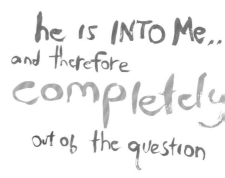

he is INTO Me.. and therefore completely out of the question

I never give this unfortunate candidate my phone number, let alone a chance. I am nice, but merely cordial. I am suspicious of him. He scares me. Clearly there is something broken in him. He must have a mental problem if he can't see what is so obviously wrong with me!

The second guy is charming, attractive and obviously interested. It

takes weeks to know him. We flirt on occasion and I wonder if he will

ever ask me out. He finally does, and predictably he has some kind

of problem: He's a workaholic; he travels 52 of 56 weeks a year; he

lives in another state; he's an alcoholic or substance abuser; he is

emotioinally flawed, shut-down or in some other way pre-occupied.

He likes me, but he is unavailable.

This means even if he professes to be thoroughly in love, there is

always something keeping him at at arm's length.

This is my man. If he asks for my number, I'll give him a shot!

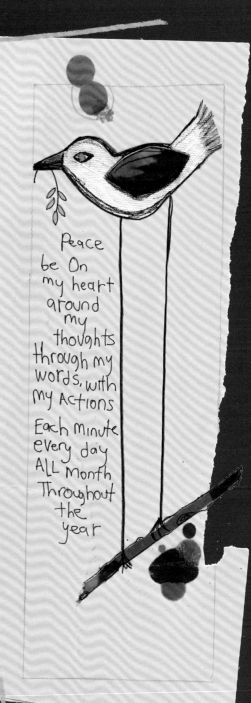

Peace be On my heart around my thoughts through my words, with my Actions Each minute every day ALL month Throughout the year

He is more than a date. He is a project.

I have wondered for years, "WHY am I attracted to such men?" Do I have

a sick way of needing to get approval from barren resources? Now as I sit

here and examine it more closely, I wonder: do I choose unavailable men

deliberately, because they are safe? Has my defensiveness brought me to

this? Am I the one who's afraid of commitment?

Unavailable = low risk. Wow! This resonates like a physical shock. I can't

escape the possibility.

I Laughed
when I
realized How
many years it
took to discover
who I am
...by first
zealously
exploring...
Who I am not

If this is true, then would it be a crazy

leap to assume that I am also unavailable?

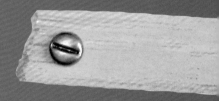

As I start to dig, and dig deep, I know it must be true.

It's strange to admit, but the unavailable guy gives *me* an out. I can cry and carry on about his distraction, but I am not called upon to play "big girl" either. I can be funny and sarcastic and jaded and hide behind his problems and never have to face my own. I don't have to give 100% of myself and risk the ultimate rejection of having tried and failed again.

Never having been forced to courageously choose yes, I hide miserably in maybe. One foot is jammed in the exit door, bruised and bleeding, but ready at all times to move.

The truth of this exercise is ultimately this: the un-available man doesn't have a chance. For years we can play this game of "come here — go away." I am good at this. I work myself to death to win him over. I give him plenty of space. I pretend to be indifferent and aloof. The moment he starts to yield, I get suspicious and kick him squarely in the teeth. When he leaves, I'm devastated; if he stays, I'm in a panic and paralyzed with fear.

So we start the cycle over again. How much can he take?

I am the bridge, the gatekeeper and the wall.

I create what I defend against.

I am terrified of being left again, so I will force him to leave.

I'm afraid I won't see it coming so I'm hyper-vigilant... and sly.

I must be in charge!

What a no-fun game. It has kept me spinning, crying, neurotic, obsessive, and heartbroken for years. I can only imagine the no-thrill on the other side, for the men who've attempted to love me. The good time, party girl isn't really that much fun.

I've hurt more than one unsuspecting male by letting him through a crack in the door and then slamming it in his face!

Is this some deviant form of human nature? Do we do that – look past the available sources of love in front of us because they are too easy? Are we always grasping for the unattainable? Do we continually chase what we perceive to be an upgrade?

Or, is it just *my* nature?

I want to change this. I want to heal this part of me. I want to learn to trust love again but I don't know how. I will start by apologizing to my date of the other night. He is not available, but he is kind and doesn't deserve to be beaten-up.

When did I become this person, this crusty, insecure mess? When I was married, my single friends came to me for advice. I was the Mrs. Brady of the dating world, the wise married one. Now, the very same people look at me as if I've regressed to age 16. I am the, oh, so cheesy Sandy in *Grease*; completely obsessed but singing "better shape up" in my hot pants.

I will let "Mr. Unavailable" go. I will not breathe life into this going-nowhere scenario.

I won't weird him out with my overwhelming "We need to talk" summit. A simple apology will do.

But if I lose myself and go overboard, at least I will walk away with the relief of knowing I have been real. I hope he will feel some relief, too.

I look forward to moving deliberately toward a healthier place; a place where I can

confidently look available love straight in the eye and feel worthy of its offer.

I want to have the courage to talk and invite it in. Or at the very least, when it

asks, give it my phone number.

OK, OK!

I won't give up everything.

ILL Wear the sweet hot pants, too.

thank god for the great friend ... that may see 'it' coming

but still provides a soft place to fall

Angry

"What counts is not necessarily the size of the dog in the fight. It's the size of the fight in the dog."

-Dwight D. Eisenhower

Aww, isn't that nice?

My sarcastic inner voice sneers inside my head as I look at the

perfect people buying their perfect organic produce... with their

perfectly clean babies tucked into their perfect, hiking-ready

backpacks. My eyes narrow angrily. What a perfect way to spend

a perfect Saturday morning.

I recognize I'm in real trouble when I fume over the people

picking out pumpkins when it's only September.

By the time I'm through judging the innocent people at the

farmers' market, I've progressed from irritated to pissed off and

now, simply mean-spirited and hateful.

Honestly, those people buying carrots? detail of life neatly labeled in color-coded Tupperware. People

Have I sunk that low? who actually get their leaves to the curb on yard waste pick-up

I judge the obvious just as diligently. You day. People whose kids are dressed in clean fashionable clothes.

know... those couples at sporting events People who eat healthy, organic snacks and plan after school

where Mom and Dad are both present. play dates. Those folks have long been the objects of my

They've been on my radar for years, along deepening resentment. These are the ones who, in my past life,

with the moms who seem to have every closely resembled me.

F O

I think of them as I stare at the gaping hole in my screen door. I

don't fixate on that particular screen, because it is just a talisman;

a representative of the other screens within my house that have

holes in them. It represents one more thing I can't seem to get to.

I know enough to recognize I'm clearly out of balance. My

rancid judgments of innocent people are just a projection of the

judgments and anger I have toward myself, yadda, yadda... I know

this, and yet I am still simmering.

What am I really angry about? Simmering hotly on the surface is

only the tip of the iceberg. Dig, dig...

naked
and on my
knees

years
of good
enough
were callously
stripped away

an Angel
took mercy and
held my hand

'Fear not my
Love'

'good' was merely
insulating you
from
Vastly great.

KB

I'm angry that I'm doing this alone.

I'm angry it doesn't appear to be getting easier.

I'm angry my life took a detour into hell and the world didn't stop and wait for me to recover.

I'm angry I'm one bookend trying to keep a stack of wobbly books together with no support at the other end.

I'm angry I fail miserably, and regularly.

I'm angry when people don't cut me any slack.

I'm angry when people think of me as handicapped and cut me too much slack.

I'm angry my love relationship has ended yet again.

I'm angry I got involved with him, that I chose another person who withdraws into an abyss when stressed.

I'm angry I had to break up with him and I'm angry that he let me.

I'm angry I feel abandoned.

I'm angry I have so much to do, with so little help.

I'm angry my kids don't have their father around.

I'm angry my son has to have surgery and he is only three.

I'm angry my father's cancer is back.

I'm angry my aunt has cancer too.

I'm angry at anyone who is laughing, smiling, or feeling good.

I'm angry at everyone who has friends, because I feel increasingly alone.

I'm angry because my life used to be good.

I'm angry I have everything I need, and still can't figure out how to be happy.

I'm angry because my nine year old daughter has a FUCKING DISEASE that is out of control, and I am angry that I can't fix it.

I'm angry because God didn't get the memo to KEEP MY KIDS OUT OF IT.

I'm more than angry with God. I'm furious at the concept that there is one.

There is a great, big, beautiful world out there, and I can't

see it or bring it inside. I feel like an empty shell. I can't

feel anything... except fire.

I'm afraid I will get
stuck in despair.

there came a
time
when the freedom
of release
eclipsed the
burdon of fury...
because forgiveness
was so much
lighter and full
of possibility

Camp Dakota

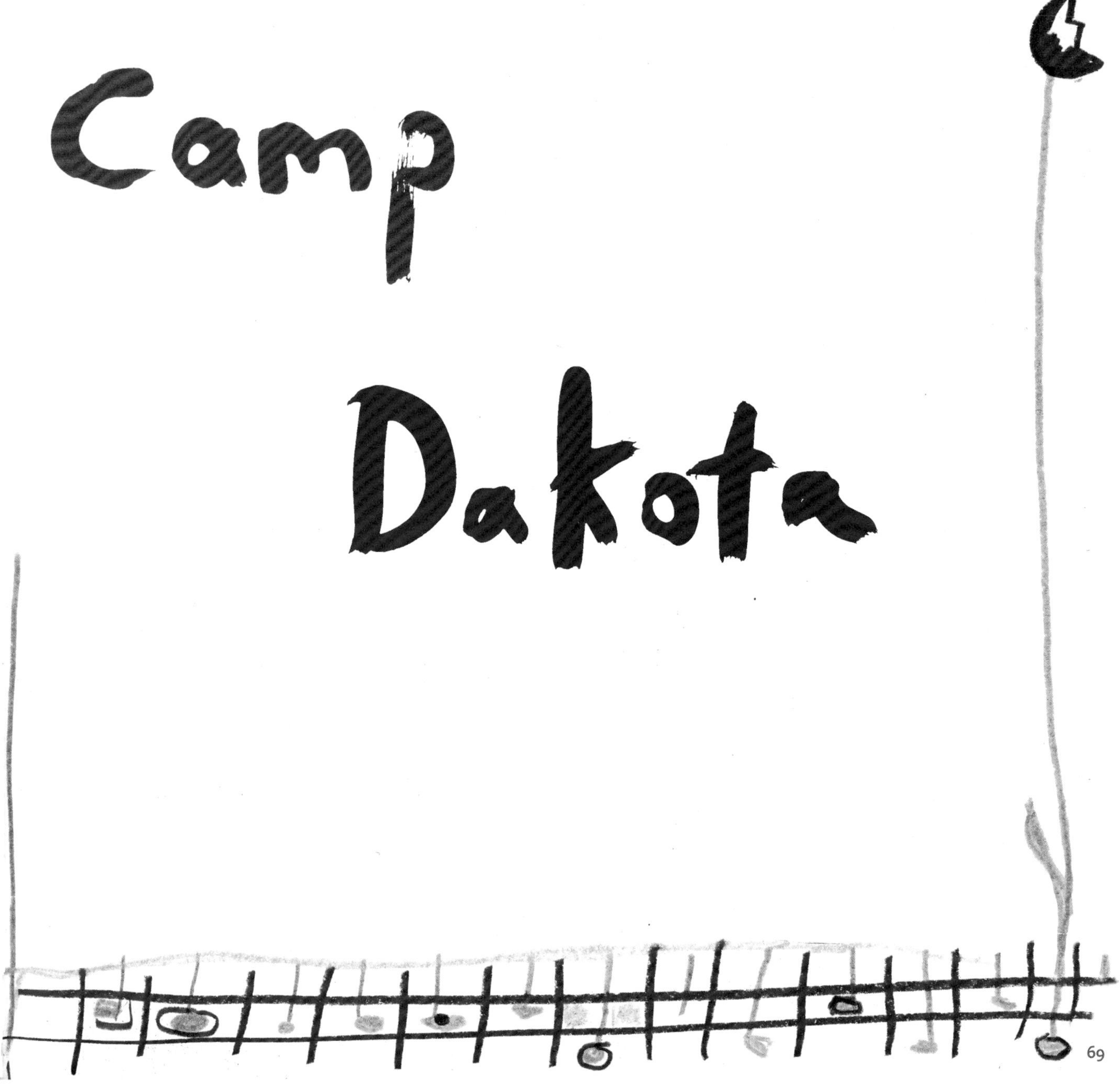

Today I dropped Mia off at her first overnight camp, a camp for kids with Rheumatoid Arthritis.

The trip to Lapeer was pretty quiet... I think we were all nervous. We listened to Anya's Ipod and

sang songs from Wicked. Anya and I took turns reassuring Mia she was going to have a great

time (dually convincing her and ourselves). I was anxious about the entire thing and hadn't been

sleeping. Anya was anxious, too. She's more than a big sister. she is a form of co-parent

Earlier she had an opportunity to forego the ten- hour drive but chose instead to come; she wasn't

going to miss this for anything. Both of us were more than curious about what lay ahead.

For weeks I'd been trying to unscramble the source of my tension. By sending her to this camp, I

was admitting that Mia in fact has an auto immune disease. We are technically joining the ranks

of the disabled. Even writing this makes me uneasy. I've explained the situation to our inner circle,

our "tribe," but I haven't met any kids or their parents who are dealing with this.

We haven't joined the JRA foundation or participated in any local, "Walk for the Cure" events. We have been "visiting" this disease (which is easy to do when Mia looks so unaffected). This was just going to be a side trip – one we were enduring as an interim measure.

We have been squatters, not people shopping for permanant real estate on the corner of helpless and disabled. Our visit would be brief.

Denial for me has been tenatious and steadfast.

The fact is – I am sending my daughter to a camp for special needs kids at the recommendation of her doctor and she has been accepted. Nobody is rejecting her, sending her back or saying, "You were misdiagnosed; it really isn't that bad."

She fits in.

It is so very hard to digest.

I am angry that I'm doing this alone. I am angry that I will once again be summoned by her father to be the eyes

and ears of such a personal experience. I feel like I am always the leader who clears the path and survives.

As we approach Camp Dakota, I'm feeling more and more apprehensive. What will the camp be like? What will

the kids be like? I told Mia the kids are just like her. I faked it; I don't know that and secretly fear they are not. I

suspect they will be weird, strange, and un-relatable. They are probably not as smart as Mia, or as athletic.

The judgments were rampant and ludicrous when observed.

Three hours into our trip, we turned onto a dirt road. A plastic corrugated yard sign was stuck in the dirt:

"Arthritis Foundation Camp Dakota." It was official. Mia started to get antsy. We all did. I followed a Honda

Pilot down the bumpy road, and was relieved it was a normal car. A normal car? Was I expecting a burnt-out,

dilapitated rust bucket? A spaceship full of weirdos? I wondered what the parents inside the car were like.

When we finally entered camp, a large sign appeared at the entrance:

"Camp Dakota, a Special Camp for Kids with Disabilities."

I sucked in my breath and sped past the sign so Anya and Mia wouldn't see it.

There is was in full sight: the "D" word

I tried desperately to dis-jar my rigid shoulders from around my earlobes.

A teenage counselor met us in the parking lot and immediately put us at ease. We piled Mia's bag and sleeping

pack next to "THE PINES" sign (the cabin she was assigned to), and met another girl who was staying in her

cabin. She was adorable. She didn't appear to have a third head or additional limbs. Her family looked pretty

average, too.

We made our way to the registration lodge. Inside were dozens of normal-looking families with normal-looking

kids. Their clothes were fashionable, as if purchased within the last five years. Where on earth did I derive my

stereotype? A stereotype I didn't recognize until that very moment.

Why was I shocked that the families looked just like us? Or that we looked just like them?

Why did I think the scene would resemble an episode of mork and mindy at a refugee camp?

I subconsciously expected rainbow suspenders and grubby, collarless tee shirts. I expected a group

of displaced misfits in a third world setting of decades ago.

These people, the ones in the room, were my contemporaries.

What made me think cruel diseases happen only to uneducated, un-savvy, poor families? To

parents who let their kids eat potato chips and drink orange soda for breakfast? To families that

are somehow negligent and secretly deserving? Where on earth did I acquire the belief that somehow

we were above this? That we were too smart, or good, or elite, or holy?

Have the Jongens been living in a bubble? A time warp?

Where did I get such a harsh, judgmental perspective? Ms. Department of Peace, Ms. Soul Soup,

Ms. Love is Bigger? She has been tossing judgment around like a javelin.

I thought the same thing about head lice. Only dirty kids got it... until my own three very dirty kids

got it and we couldn't get rid of it for three months!

There were a couple of kids in wheelchairs, but they looked normal, too. Just kids – without scales

or antennae as far as I could see; just little people who couldn't walk. They were kids with braids and

glasses and crooked teeth and freckles and untied shoes; kids listening to Ipods and playing hand-

held video games as they waited in line. There were parents with combination expressions just like

mine: exhaustion, relief, excitement, nervousness.

As I waited in line to see the medic and schedule Mia's daily medications,

I scanned the scene and quickly did a mental 180. I joined an instant

"us." The parents each held large, gallon-size ziplock baggies with

labeled bottles of medicine, injections, liquids, pills and other paraphernalia.

Illness is not so secret-secret here. My refrigerator houses the same medicines.

The only thing that set this apart from any other camp was the thing that pulled us together: our kids were sick. Those baggies contained all the fear, tension and worry of every parent in the room. They represented visits to a pediatrician, pediatric rheumatologist, ophthalmologist, physical therapist, occupational therapist, dietician, nephrologist, neurologist, gastroenterologist, cardiologist, pulmonologist, orthopedic surgeon, dentist and monthly blood screenings.

But at this moment, all fear and tension was happening on the inside. Except for a few kids with joint braces and a few in wheelchairs, illness went unnoticed. And somehow, in this setting, it became clear that even an antennae or two wouldn't be a big deal. They were all kids and we are all human.

So, as my daughter had her first experience away from home, we joined a new world – a world that is safe for her; a world that understands her; a world where she (and we) can meet others going through the same things.

as it turns out, I have been the One in the bubble

I have been in the refugee camp, angry with God for making me feel isolated, picked-on and betrayed. I have been Mama Bear at her worst: ferocious, screaming, and enraged at the attack on her innocent cub.

As we begin to embrace this disease and the extended family that goes with it, there is solace within its walls – not at the perimeter. After a year of running, cursing and blaming, the peace I have been looking for rests within. It is a place where our family can look truth straight in the eye and instead of being horrified, feel mercy. And in that moment, lay down our armor and rest in its arms.

We
We a[...]
hippie[...]
Survivor[...]
french[...]
rigid

We are Proud, humble and
gay and straight, wearing yamakas
We are hunters and Vegans (ar[...]
and peaceful) We are Brave
a Country Connected by hope[...]
We have not forgotten we are f[...]

ve not forgotten who we are
adicals-wise, blonde and nappy
green and eager
nd Cowboys-We are native and new
heroes, fit and in wheelchairs. We are
es and Sushi, dreamers and Scientists
d bent Suits and clergy, temples and churches
STILL Learning ♥ We Love BIG
nd sombraros, kimonas and Locks
ll inclusive buffet of the rowdy
e are the world collected in
We are awake and on fire
to say We are Americans

About
time

In flight school there are two approaches to a student's first solo. One is to set a date and give the student plenty of prep time. The other is to realize the student will only use that mental time to stress out and undermine her own efforts.

One day you're comfortably going over maneuvers with your trusty flight instructor (with whom you have created an intimate bond), and he casually steps out of the plane and says, "You are on your own." In an absolute panic, you think he must be kidding! You can't believe he would trust you with a life and death operation. But he is serious. It's time to cut the cord. You're prepared, but have become dependent.

It is time to spread your wings and do what you came here to do.

God treats me like this.

When prayers are answered for me, I'm usually in a bathrobe, shoveling snow with one hand, while changing a baby diaper with the other. I have not had my first cup of coffee. An opportunity presents itself and I don't have my act together. I haven't showered, and I have bad roots. My lessons come in sweatsuit moments when I'm totally unprepared.

A prayer that pleads, "Please teach me to be unafraid," is answered by an apprehension-building, five credit college course in flight training – during the most tumultuous months of my life. A prayer that offers, "I want to do your work," places me squarely in front of my City Commission, in a snow storm, on behalf of the Department of Peace legislation. A prayer that begs, "Please grant me strength,"

has me learning how to give my ten year old daughter medical injections. All at the same time.

Am I merely unsuspecting, or perfectly primed?

I don't know the answer.

fly

Maybe I should spend less time in sweats.

When our state coordinator for the Peace Alliance suggested I be our district representative, I questioned her sanity. I questioned my ability. I questioned my schedule and my time commitment. "*I am a single mother after all,*" I thought, with a trace of incredulousness.

four short months later, I found myself sitting face to face with my congressman

Like my flight instructor, little angels have come along to give me

a loving, but forceful push. There is a part of me that will hide

"in training" forever. Especially with the big stuff.

I know there is a place of balance.
I'm just not claiming to have it yet.

There appear to be two different types of growth. The first is a

place where angels appear and give you an

uncomfortable push past your hurdles.

The second is a traditional place where growth is granted over time. This is new for me. It is a place where experience acts as a catalyst for wonderful opportunities. For example, I have been in business for five years, laying groundwork. I have paid my dues and have been tenacious. I have worked very hard. Now, galleries come to find me. That is a wonderful place to be. It cannot be rushed. It cannot be forced.

But even in that space, every single time a major player has contacted me, I have been unprepared. I have been tired, rude, presumptuous, or distracted. I have never seen it coming, nor ushered them in with a dazzling smile.

Miracles always catch me off-guard.

I have had brutal arguments with God.

Plenty of them.

I agreed to go to school. I agreed to be a student, but I didn't sign up for the advanced course.

I said I wanted to live
a BIG Life.
I didnt say
I wanted to be
the poster child
for being catapulted
full throttle.

Last week I scrambled to get to my flight lesson. Hap-hazard and harried

as I was, my worries started to dissolve as I did the mandatory steps

in a preflight check, like sumping the pumps and checking the oil. By

the time we were ready to take off, I was in full flight mode. It takes so

much concentration for me to maneuver an airplane, it clears my mind.

There's not enough capacity to obsess over all the other worries I have.

Shutting down the aircraft after my lesson, I looked at my instructor and smiled. I don't think flight

schools know this, but even the scariest, most uptight instructor lends a validating energy to the student.

My instructors calm me down. Even though we may try each other's patience and my skills might seem

questionable, the cause is not.

"Well, I wouldn't say
I was in the 'great class',
but I had a great time
while I was trying to be
great."

– Harry S. Truman

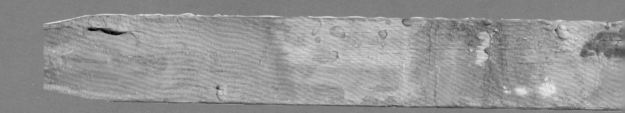

88

Flight instructors are supportive in one consistent way, and different from anyone else in my life; they don't

think wanting to fly is stupid.

I ended the day's training thinking that attempting flight in real life might always look like this. Is the timing ever

right? No major transformation in my life including flight training, has ever been planned. I have occasionally

been coached by others, but mostly the universe shoves me into the driver's seat.

It must be the only way I learn. I am a vocational hands-on student. My own voice questions, "Now?"... and it is

simply reactive, for the sake of hearing my own soprano. My gut already knows the answer.

the book is written.
It has been written.

"And the day came when the risk to remain
tight in the bud was more painful than the risk
it took to blossom."
– Anais Nin

standing
in the light
doesn't require
a sturdy spine.

Just a courageous
Soul

Willing to turn
and face
the Sun

I'm sending the first chapter to my editor today and will begin the process. I am going to

share the sordid, chaotic struggles of the past few years and hope it means something

to someone besides me.

It is time.

"Now?"

"Yes," says the robe wearing lady.

Now.

"Every blade of grass has its angel that bends over it and whispers,

'Grow, grow.'"

– The Talmud

Why is it STILL so hard to Let go?

May 2, 2005

The layers of letting go continue for me. I struggle with just "how far" I want to

let something go. I have been consciously trying to get my mind to let go of its

obsessive tendancies. It is uncomfortable. I am tempted to call or email, or engage

in some way to keep him close. We haven't talked in weeks. I am not avoiding or

ignoring. This is different. It is walking in a different direction, and I am letting

it. I don't want to watch with a clenched heart. I don't want to secretly hope he

will turn around. That is counter the point. I want to freely let him walk his walk and go about my own journey. I want to trust. I want the energy from me to be accepting and open, not longing. It is difficult. He has never been so far. On occasion his pace slows down. He looks back and accuses me "Why aren't you coming after me?"

Not this time. I will sit. I will try to avoid compulsive eating (three popsicles later.) When I am vulnerable, I will repress the urge to cling. To run after. To beg, convince and remind. Of course, that is not what I want. It is not what I need. Don't we all want a love that is running towards us with the same speed? My stomach wrenches and I move forward, creating a space for repose and ultimately freedom.

I believe | leap | soar

soul mate

The past few years have been rough. Life has handed me a steady stream of challenges and disappointments, and with them an unfortunate build-up of self loathing. For example, while on the phone with a girlfriend the other day, she said in exasperation, "God, just stop it!" as I detailed another round of my idiotic mis-adventures.

I've always been somewhat self-critical, but lately it has turned extreme. I am sick of these toxic out-pourings and exhausted from my negative self-berating.

"How could you let this happen?" I admonish myself. "You know better. You're acting like a fool!"

I've begun reading, The Four Agreements by Don Miguel Ruiz. The first chapter hit me between the eyes. "In your whole life, nobody has every abused you more than you have abused yourself."

Reading further, "And the limit of your self-abuse is exactly the limit that you will tolerate from someone else."

Then, "If someone abuses you a little more than you abuse yourself, you will probably walk away from that person. If someone abuses you a little less than you abuse yourself, you will probably stay in that relationship and tolerate it endlessly."

All of this left me reeling as I recalled my own past.

I am at a fortunate place in my learning, where I believe most of the answers lie within me (we just need to find each other). My spiritual studies have led me from novice-seeker to somewhere in the middle of self-knowledge. I have thought, analyzed, read, worked, and therapized myself to death.

It feels like I've been on this journey for hundreds of years! The solution is

not going to come from any outside source. I need to implement a plan for

self-love *from* myself, *to* myself.

So how and where do I start?

What about my *self* feels depleted, desperate, and out of balance? What do I

need most? Affection and attention top the list. Can I provide these things

to myself?

Hmmm...

What if I had a love
affair with myself?

I gulped a laugh and coffee came out my nose.

oh my God,
that sounds so
Gloria
Stienem!
Will I be chanting
to my vagina next?

As I started to think about a plan, a smile crept across my face. I can kill two birds

with one stone. I can get the warm fuzzies I so desperately want, and give them to

myself at the same time. I am both the giver and the receiver. I can't lose!

This could be the most asinine thing I've ever done. I devised a plan. I thought about

all the places where sweet nothings might suddenly appear.

My cell phone has a massive void that needs to be filled. Like a Pavlov dog, I salivate

when my text – message alarm goes off. A message! A sweet nothing!

SO – what if I started texting myself? I blushed. "Is this totally pathetic?" I thought,

as I figured out how to plug my own cell phone number into my address book.

What happened was surprising. The ringer went off. I paused for a few moments, and

then opened the message as if it was fresh and unexpected.

"Kristen. I love you. I love you!"

Big fat tears welled up in my eyes. Seeing this message blink across the screen made me smile. I replied, "I love you too," and the message was returned to me!

"I think you are beautiful without make-up," was the next one. I smiled.

"Oh, thanks!" was my reply.

I instantly started to feel a lift.

"Honey, everything will be alright," soothes a weary soul.

As of today, the experiment continues. I avoid anything explicit. But, "I luv ur hot bod!" is not off limits. Reminding my single self that I am not becoming a man is a core part of my recovery.

I take heat from my friends for the mischievous smile I'm wearing as I check my cell phone. They wonder who the mystery lover is.

I found my Soulmate
after a long arduous search.
I wasnt trying my best. On
my knees again, Pathetic
and drunk from cup
after cup of humility.
I was everything the Love
doctors dont recommend. this
and Long Came
Savior, this gentle Soul who
prayed with me. I felt seen
I felt heard. I felt grateful
that my self loathing retreted.
I am no Longer afraid of
commitment I believe in
this Affair. It is A Love that
is whole and stable

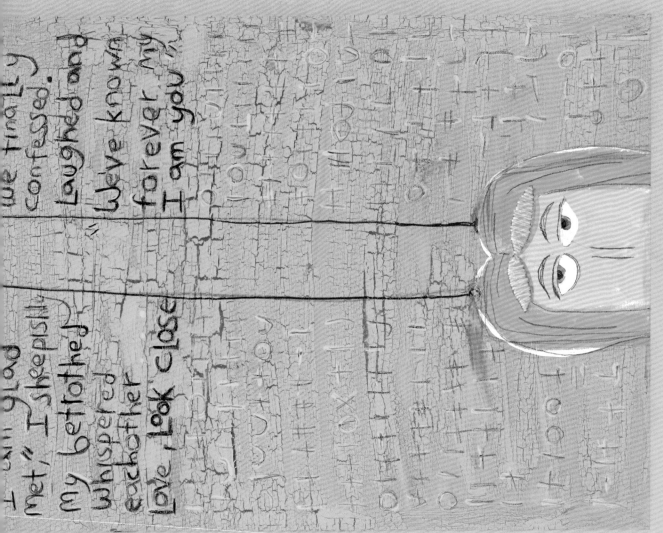

I am glad met," I sheepishly confessed. "We finally laughed and My betrothed, whispered We've known each other forever, my love, look close I am you?"

"I'll bet She'd look great in that tee shirt," I say, as I buy her a little token

of my love. I might send her flowers too. I definitely need to remind

her I think she's courageous (She was feeling insecure yesterday). She

never gets real paper mail so I think I'll send her one of those funny,

inspirational cards.

Since doing this experiment, I've been strangely at ease. I feel good about

something that can't disappear, evaporate, or get bored with itself. I will

always have an interest in Me, and I will always be everywhere with Her.

She knows when I need support, and when I need space. We are always

on the same page. She wants sushi when I want sushi! She wants to go

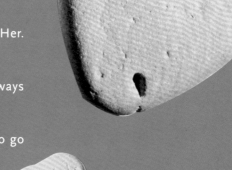

out when I want to go out! She wants to lay low when I want to lay low. We agree on everything! She says

outlandish things sometimes, but I always know where She's coming from.

I practice not taking Her so seriously. When She takes a wrong turn, I am there. I stand next to Her

when it's time to kick ass. I have Her back and She has mine. We are working on trust. I am certain it

will come with time.

I notice myself smiling more. I have more patience with my

teenager. I hug my little guy a lot. I am writing. I have more

compassion for my emotional 10 year old. I am enjoying the

heck out of my new dog, Darma, and I smile at the girl in the

mirror. She's not that bad. In fact, She's kind of cute.

There goes my ringer.

It's her again.
She's so attentive.

She must be feeling frisky.

Journal, June 12, 2006

Risking love again

I thought I'd worked it all out. The years of introspection, dialog and emotional micromanagement convinced me I knew the

score. The mistakes of my marriage were quantifiable, like so many specimens in a Petri dish.

Now I find myself teetering on wobbly legs... I'm so afraid what I thought I learned won't help me now.

I'm in a relationship that is exactly what I asked for. Enough space for me to live my life without being swallowed-up whole.

Enough passion to fill two rooms. Everything I want... and yet I am miserable. The fear that surrounds my heart is crippling me.

I am afraid of letting myself trust.

I am afraid of getting attached.

I am afraid of appearing needy.

I am afraid I am getting in too deep.

I am afraid of being left.

I am afraid all of these fears are irrelevant because, ultimately, it is too late.

As honest and raw as my personality appears on the outside, there is a secret layer; a hidden chamber so full of insecurities it tortures me from the inside-out. Since my divorce, my barometer hasn't been working. I don't know when I'm holding on too tightly or thrusting a worthy suitor away too hastily. I don't know when a relationship is worth the effort it takes to move forward.

Here's my second chance, and I don't want to blow it again.

I've been through a series of slash and burn romances; passionate affairs that had no chance of succeeding. I was in control, and he was attracted to me. Those two things were all that mattered. I held the knife and I lit the match. In a short time, I have become an expert at the capture and release game of man hunting.

Now, there is a Real Contender. He sneaked up from behind when I wasn't looking. I was feeling so sure of myself, when he came along and swept me off my feet.

I am unprepared and unraveled. I want to be in control. I'm terrified of being misunderstood. I'm afraid he will see the real me, the terrified little girl… and leave. He will think I am too much: too needy, too insecure, too screwed up, too jaded, too difficult, too desperate, and too pathetic.

There is so much that is out of my hands.

I am not the confident girl I used to be, and I want her back.

The girl who didn't fret about everything. She trusted.

She jumped in head first and assumed it would all work out.

She said things to guys like, **"If you can find someone better, go for it."**

Go for it?! Was I crazy... or just sure of my own worth? Now I spend shallow moments managing my insecurities. I position myself so I won't look fat. When did I become this person, this ridiculous mess? I never used to get jealous. Now I need constant reassurance.

On a daily basis I think, "I'm going to break off this relationship and regain control. I need to put an end to the misery."

Not because I don't love him. I don't want to lose him. My insecurities spill upon me from every direction. I'm drowning in them!

I know that there are only two ultimate outcomes. One is where we get married; the other is we break up. I am terrified of both.

(Is there someplace in between, a place to just "be," a place to rest?)

As I process this stream of nightmarish head games, I know I can run; I do have control over that. I can self-protect and withhold my feelings. I can decide I am not ready to commit, hide, and work this out later. Or, I can slowly open up and risk love again.

I am afraid. she whispered one
last time. Me too. he said softly
And with that he placed all of the
fearful no's in a tight ball behind
them, and took her hand. They
each moved forward, ever so
gently, quietly committing to
discover... all
the miraculous
wonders
of
yes

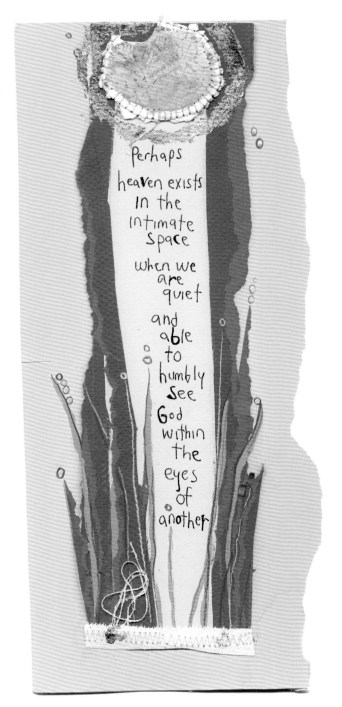

Perhaps
heaven exists
in the
intimate
space
when we
are
quiet
and
able
to
humbly
see
God
within
the
eyes
of
another

"Your current
safe boundaries
were once
unknown
frontiers"

– Anonymous

Van and the plastic Pants

It's funny to look back through the train wreck of your life and see yourself even worse off than you are now. For over five years I've been single and raising my kids on my own. At first it was a scramble just to keep us assembled and sheltered. We set up shop on a stack of cards. I got the kids registered for school. Found a place to live. Financed the house. Gave birth to baby Van. Found an office space, etc., etc., etc. It was an everyday push dealing with movers, service people, utilities, and septic-tank cleaners to name a few, in order to rebuild our lives quickly.

Freshly divorced, I felt miserable and anxious. The last thing I wanted to do was scare new neighbors with a clear view of an unkempt bomb site. More than anything I wanted to appear together. In the end, it's ridiculous trying to cover-up. I reeked of chaos. Vacant black hole eyes and a noticeable twitch made *crazy* impossible to miss.

One particular spring, my son Van was three – a time when he became fond of escaping the family compound. Chez Jongen apparently held little value or inspiration for him. Managing my household was (and still is) a difficult task that changed from day to day like shifting sand.

One morning in a desperate attempt to jump start my life (again) I got up early and went to the gym. All the kids were asleep, including my babysitter/daughter, Anya.

On this particularly chilly morning Van heard my car pull away, let himself out of his crib in his diaper and left the house. He thought he was being abandoned. He cried all the way down my road, around the bend, and up the hill bawling, "I want my Mama!" Cars were driving by, and one of my neighbors came out of her house when she saw him. The little guy was a good distance from home.

She knew him from previous sightings, and placed several phone calls around the neighborhood and finally to my home – calls the sleeping girls ignored. She came up to the house and rang the doorbell 15 times (also ignored by the girls) before I drove up. Suddenly, the girls miraculously awoke, and we all converged on my front porch.

Naked little Vanny jumped on me with his tear-soaked cheeks.

The woman was not impressed. I was furious with the girls. She thought Van had been left home alone... another notch on the tree of humiliation.

As spring turned into summer, Van continued his wanderlust to neighbors' homes while

I was watering the plants or doing outside chores. In a flash he'd be gone! I would have

to yell for him, again embarrassing myself. These people are my neighbors, not my family

or inner circle. They are cordial and polite, but naturally they don't want a three year old

begging for doughnuts at 7:30 in the morning. I could never seem to keep tabs on him...

Vanny loved being an escape artist.

My kids added to the impression of parental neglect by always seeming to

look homeless. With closets full of nice clothes, they repeatedly chose the

holey, ill fitting rags from the garage sale box.

My neighborhood is wonderful. It is safe. It feels good. It is essentially a

Beaver-Cleaver hood. That is the attraction. And that is where I get into

trouble. I am not a Beaver Cleaver gal. I always feel four steps behind the

normalcy curve.

The coup de gras came one summer morning when my neighbor Jackie called to let me

know Van was once again in her yard. "What?" I stammered. This was the fourth time

this summer. He was sitting on her front steps chatting away. Jackie was chuckling,

and I was trying to hide my humiliation. Mia was out playing in the neighborhood, even

though the last thing I'd asked her to do was to get him dressed. But she was in a hurry

to play, and bustled out the door. Van was still in the house when I last saw him.

Why was he always escaping? Why didn't I ever know? Why was I always surprised? My

ego was once again marinating in humility. I didn't even want to show my face, I was

so embarrassed; so I sent Anya down to get him.

Sometimes It takes only one clear voice in a sea of loud chatter to rise above the chaos and shift the planet back to center

It was shockingly worse that I'd thought. Up the driveway came

Anya and Van, hand in hand. Anya looked supremely annoyed.

Van happily chugged up the long drive, wearing only a pair of

clear-plastic training pants. Where did she find those? They were

the kind one uses over cloth diapers – with elastic on the tummy

and legs. Nope, no cloth diaper there... just the rubber pants. His

little penis was pushed up against the clear wall of the vinyl.

"Oh, my God!" I gasped, running down the driveway.

"Oh, it gets better," Anya said dryly and turned him around. He

had pooped in the plastic pants and sat down on their porch,

leaving a brown patty showcased in the rearview window. He

stunk to high heaven. I wanted to die.

Van is four and a half now and rarely takes off like he used to, but my humility is still at ready-alert.

The old Chestnut, "What will the neighbors think?" has a defeated, stale air about it. The neighbors

already think, a lot.

It's a good thing our house is tucked back a distance from the rest. People don't really get what I do.

They say things like, "She's a 'writer,'" using finger quotes or, an "artist," with raised eyebrows. People

shake their heads as I drive by in my little compact car with a Great Dane hanging out the window, a

teenager covering her face in the front seat and two fighting kids in the back. We look like a family of

gypsies in a clown car. Why? I was simply trying to save gas.

But the image of Van in his plastic pants... Van in his dirty little clear-plastic pants is one I will never,

ever forget. Poor Jackie. She probably won't either.

Nip tuck

I am sprawled in a patch of sunlight on my deck, trying not to miss a single ray of warmth. It feels

like a peek at redemption after a formidable winter. I think the residents of Northern Michigan

(myself included) are starting to show signs of wear and tear. Baggy eyes and desperate glances

abound. We are a snow-sodden tribe of warriors who've taken a beating from the white stuff, heavy

grey-clouds and more white stuff. Winter lasted three months too long this year and only sunshine

will redeem us.

I have the day to myself and for the first time in months I'm not pulled in 75 directions. My cell

phone is (gasp!) turned off. I am lying on a sun-streaked piece of carpet, trying to calm myself.

My upcoming surgery has me thoughtful and completely stressed-out. It feels like a giant chapter in my life is about to pass through on its way to oblivion. I hesitate to even write about it.

The moment I realized I could have my stomach fixed (as in, I actually had the power to do something about this) I was awestruck. I was vacationing with my friend Heather and having the usual pre-bathing suit panic in our hotel room. She asked me why I never wear a bikini. I looked at her as if she was nuts.

In fact, I asked, "Are you nuts?"

We were in Hawaii, far away from home, but I NEVER revealed my stomach to ANYONE! It is a huge, self-conscious knot of anxiety. Maybe it was the sun, or the Mai Tai's, or maybe it was a need to show someone what was going on in my tormented mind; but something got into me. I turned to show her my secret. I pulled out all the skin like silly putty. Her eyes widened.

"Exactly" I muttered.

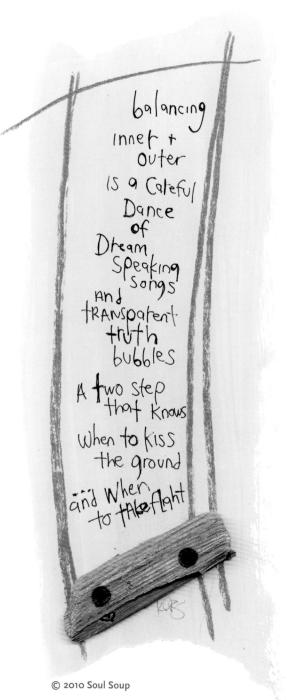

balancing
inner +
outer
is a careful
Dance
of
Dream
Speaking
songs
and
transparent
truth
bubbles

A two step
that knows
when to kiss
the ground
and when
to take flight

© 2010 Soul Soup

"Why don't you just get a tummy tuck?" she asked,

innocently enough.

"Yeah, right," was my response.

"Why not?" she asked again. She was serious.

"Because they cost, like, a million dollars, and I just

don't know..." I rebuffed, feigning a new interest in

my suitcase.

I'd considered a tummy tuck before but decided I had

to be at least 40 and should first make a dramatic

case for it. I mean, only rich people and celebrities

get plastic surgery. Heather is from L.A., she doesn't

understand how it really is. She looks fantastic and

is 6 years older than me. She was allowed to be stunning, but I was a mom. Midwesterners don't do those

things..right? I had to suck it up.

Yet the moment the thought entered my mind, and with Heather looking so certain, it became a possibility.

Why couldn't I get a tummy tuck? Why was I resigned to life as a Shar-pei? Everything else was fairly fit and

in shape, but this skin, this skin...

For the rest of our trip we talked about it. I started shyly practicing by wearing a bikini under my dress — just

to see what it felt like. Then I did a half top, half skirt incognito thing at the beach. It was quite ridiculous,

but I was becoming addicted. I wore this bikini under everything.

I decided then and there, I was going to have it done. When I got home I researched, saved and consulted.

I scheduled and then eagerly kept busy during the 6 month wait list. Between work and kids, I watched Dr.

90210 and You Tube. I read books. "Major surgery," they said, "requires at least six weeks recovery."

"They don't know me," I thought. I am a warrior.

Now it is time. I am full of fear and anticipation. So much mental space has been tied up in

this fleshy clump of cells. To rid myself of the problem seems shameless, even arrogant.

The truth is, I have felt that carrying around this scar tissue and excess skin for 17 years

was my punishment: my punishment for being irresponsible, for embarrassing myself and

my family, for the audacity to bring a child into the world at age 20.

I am not talking about a typical baby pouch here. I am talking about 6 inches of loose skin

that hides beneath my jeans. Only a few privileged people know it is there. It is my Achilles

heel. To have that cut away and removed represents more than a tummy tuck to me. It

represents layers and layers of self-belittlement. It represents a secret shame. It represents

always presenting a stiff upper lip. It represents surrendering womanhood for motherhood.

It represents a shadow cast on me and my daughter that it is time to release.

It may seem melodramatic and even shallow, but I am battling all this in my mind.

Cosmetic surgery has never been my thing. Am I becoming a narcissist? What will

people think? What will my new beau think? God, he is a naturalist and this seems,

well... plastic.

My doctor will surgically repair my abdominal wall. It is admittedly a muscular mess

from pregnancy weight gain. He will stitch the muscles back into place. This is so

that in the future my bladder doesn't fall into my uterus from the existing large hole.

Sexy.

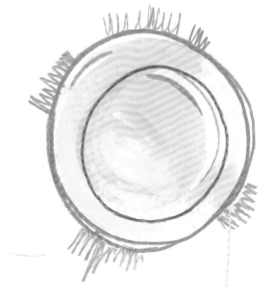

He will create a new belly button.

Weird?

He will cut away all the excess skin on my black sharpie-sketched stomach, and throw it out. Just toss it? I

wonder if it will look like chicken fat in the garbage. Is it a foot petal operated garbage can? Does the nurse

open it and mutter "Another day, another body part?"

Bizarre.

As I ponder these thoughts, the light shines intensely. It is a warm place to cuddle. My Great Dane, Darma,

is passed-out next to me. She had a bath today and is tuckered out. I can smell the rosemary, yling yling and

rose oil I added to her soap.

This surgery feels like a rite of passage, like coming out of the shadows and claiming the present. It is selfish

and only for me. It is a decision to take myself back; a decision to reunite with the Kristen I mourned the

loss of, so long ago.

It is not because I want to be 19 again – quite the opposite. It's because I want to fully embrace 36. No more

living in the past. No more guilt. I want to accept where I am at 36 without regret. Does an abdomonioplasty alone restore an eroded self esteem? Certainly not!

But it is a guilty indulgence and nice kick-start to

37 (tee-hee).

I'm feeling guilty, basking in the warmth while

the house needs cleaning and there are things to

do outside. Hopefully my life doesn't fall apart

because I didn't go outside or clean the house.

I am curled up
like a kitten in
the Sun and
it feels Wonderful

perhaps
in receiving
we heal
others
. . .
in giving
we heal
Ourselves

the Tax Man

I've spent the last three weeks in sweat pants. Since the repairmen started work on my roof I have had the urge

to purge – cleaning and throwing out garbage like a mad woman. A new roof, for some reason, makes me want to

stabilize my foundation and make the entire structure sound.

I hauled furniture from the solarium, cleaned out the basement, my art studio (with four years of dust, grime

and empty paint containers) and finally the garage. The garage was blanketed with a half-inch of sawdust from

the roofers' old plywood. I cleaned out stored fish tanks, vacuumed old couches (even using the attachments),

cleaned off bikes, and dusted crates that hauled artwork across the country. I rearranged and reevaluated junk last

observed when I moved here, four years ago.

I left Chicago in 2004, peeling away in a cloud of emotional dust that was my vaporized marriage. I packed the necessities but left behind fourteen years of documents, photographs, love letters, and other printed forms of memory. Over the years that followed, my ex-husband sifted through much of the paperwork and brought me old photos and relics.

This always annoyed me, when he placed memories in front of me like so many slaughtered lambs. I left them behind on purpose! I didn't want that life, those haunted things penetrating my safe-haven. I couldn't understand why he was forcing them on me, yet he seemed happy about it.

"Remember when..." he would start a sentence.

"Yeah, I guess," would be my unenthusiastic response.

So here I was cleaning out the garage and sorting through relics when I uncovered a crushed and musty file box covered in dust that said, "Taxes." I decide to pitch it once and for all. How did this thing get here anyway? It must have

been something he brought. I set it aside for the recycling bin, intending to dump it all.

My mind started to creep though, about identity theft – should someone see our social security numbers.

I shrugged it off and went to wipe down a scooter.

My guilty conscious forced me to return. I opened the box and looked inside. There were tax returns from

as far back as 1989. I shook my head and was poised to dump the contents of all folders into the recycling

bin – then conceded to separate the workbooks while promising to shred the returns.

I was already getting irritable at the time this was taking. Then a tiny little worm (in the giant can of

worms) I was flirting with, poked its head up and winked. My eyes eventually scanned one of the returns

and I chuckled. It was 1989, when my ex-husband worked as a landscaper. He made $2,405 for the entire

year and that summer was hit with self employment taxes. He nearly lost his mind with worry. We were newly dating, and both totally broke. He had not prepared for

taxes and was sweating bullets about how to pay them.

I skipped ahead a few years. Now it was 1993 and we were

both working for an audio visual production company. We were

"production assistants," and I laughed out loud at those returns.

My responsibilities included removing the garbage, shredding

documents and keeping the beverage fridge stocked.

It was a small but wealthy company, and we would scurry away

all the freebies we could get our hands on: broken file cabinets,

old fish tanks, anything headed for the dump was intercepted by

the garbage girl and her handy fix it boyfriend. I think we made

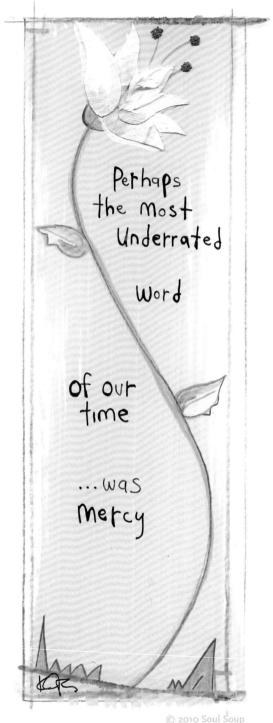

Perhaps
the most
Underrated

Word

of our
time

...was
Mercy

131

a total of eight thousand dollars that year (combined)! Our boss was a good man and gave my hubby a nice

raise when I delivered Anya (our oldest daughter.) We were still in college and stressed beyond belief.

I took a seat on the porch step and emerged four hours later.

A greeting card fell between the cracks. It was one of those fancy, formal ones. The front read, "For my

husband." I was surprised by my reaction - shocked, really. "God, I used to have a husband," I thought.

"I used to be a wife." It was so surreal to me. I have only been single

four years but it felt as odd as saying **"I am divorced."**

Back then, the smallest things caused major stress. The car needed new

brakes, and we had to scrape together money to fix them. We worked

for an entire summer fixing up a house in exchange for the owner's

old car. We refinished her wood floors and painted the interior.

Every folder was full of interesting nostalgia. God forbid, was that a WIC application? Oh my God, I WAS ON

PUBLIC ASSISTANCE! I had completely forgotten.

There was paperwork from a Hearing - because they miscalculated a doctor's bill for $300. THREE HUNDRED

DOLLARS! We missed work and toiled relentlessly about how we would pay for it if we lost the case. A pink

file containing copious notes, recordings, dated phone calls, written letters, meetings, follow up meetings,

receipts, physicians' reports, invoices and photocopies bulged at the seams. All for three hundred dollars!

Life was so difficult then. We were twenty and twenty-two, broke, and no one took us seriously.

There were tax returns from jobs I had completely forgotten about. I blush in embarrassment at how self-

important I was, considering how little I knew. There was a tax return from my hubby's first big job; a job

that had us move across the country, giddy with delight. It paid 30K and we didn't know how our family

would spend it all. During the entire trek across country we daydreamed about the things we could buy.

I called him right away and left a message. I suddenly realized where he was coming from with his boxes of photos and relics. It struck me now, how far we've come. It was all feeble nonsense back then, and took so much

scraping together. And it's funny how quickly we forget things. How the fact that I was on Medicaid and WIC

sixteen years ago somehow slipped my mind!

Spiritual guides teach the importance of staying present. "Breathing in the moment" has helped to sustain me

for years. However, this little box of history had me looking back. Step by step, my past was labeled in green,

hanging folders I bought on clearance at an office supply store. Labeled was more than a decade of clamoring,

back-sliding, crawling, growth and progress – followed by small leaps of faith. Every financial step was there,

documenting a life in motion.

I've practiced staying firmly rooted in the present, ever fearful of the avalanche that can ruthlessly sweep me into

my painful past. But this journey was different. It was a stepping backwards that steadied my foundation and

strengthened my roots. It reminded me with a solid, black and white paper trail of where I'd come from.

Those nearly-pitched papers pieced together the bones that construct my character and the musculature that holds me steady. There were the jobs that became defunct, goals that were reached, tiny measures of success and giant slides backwards; locations and friendships, homes and apartments, landlords and mortgages. They all brought me to where I am standing right now.

This trip into the past didn't derail my future. It didn't cripple me with pain. Instead, the experience reminded me not only of who I was "back then," but most importantly it created a cause for pause – a grateful checkpoint where, through a series of black and white paychecks points directly where I am today – as only the IRS can do.

to Hell and back

I have gained a lifetime of knowledge in the last five years. Many big things have gone wrong since my husband and I split up. A landslide of despair and anxiety slid down the hill and into our little family Shangri-la. Rebuilding has, and continues to be a day-by-day process in which I try to balance my center, while my ego wants to cling to the past and agonize about the future.

The tension and stress of my life had gone largely unspoken by me, but was physically visible everywhere. Continued feelings of loss and isolation were building within an overwhelming grief I couldn't express.

After the break up of my first, post-divorce relationship, I took another turn for the worse.

Our affair was on and off continually for three years. Other aspects of my personal life were

shattering, also. My dog, Babe died suddenly. She was my friend for 13 years. I am still not

over the loss of her. Then my aunt died from a brutal and cruel cancer and within six months

her mother (my Grandma) died. Six weeks later, my Grandfather (Grandma's husband of 70

years) died as well.

During that time, a couple I know (old friends from school) lost their five year old daughter

to a tragic accident in their back yard. Sadness and grief were everywhere I turned. The state

of our country in war and the great disappointment in our leadership added to feelings of

helplessness and isolation. Missing a partner, I felt I had no one to talk to about work or the

kids, or Mia's newly diagnosed disease. I felt abandoned.

I was hanging onto my sanity by my fingernails

Barely making it through the day, I was hyperventilating and having extreme panic attacks. Physically, everything hurt. The hairs on the back of my neck hurt. My heart was throbbing in agony from the dark haze suffocating my brain. I kept pushing and carpooling and working, but taking long naps because I couldn't work a full day without secretly crawling home and into bed. I began withdrawing from friends and family. My ability to cope with routine activities dwindled. I pushed. I avoided. I cried. I slept. Dread began filling my days and my family found me as despondent as I had been five years earlier.

I was fragile; Vacant

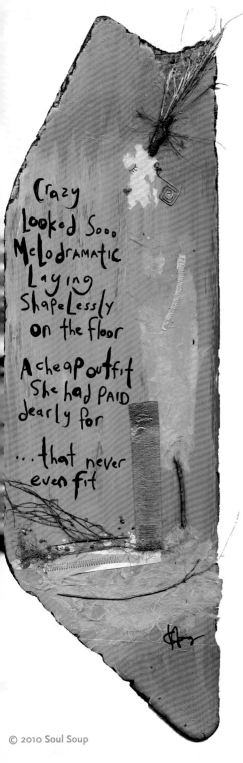

Crazy
looked Sooo
Melodramatic
Laying
Shapelessly
on the floor

A cheap outfit
She had PAID
dearly for

...that never
even fit

On a sunny October morning a year ago, I woke up feeling worse

than usual. Something was terribly wrong. Anxiety was kicking

in the walls of my mind as I wrestled panic-stricken thoughts of

the world's end. My daughter's 11th birthday was two days away!

Her Dad was coming into town too, and we were going to host a

pumpkin patch birthday party for her and her friends.

In total panic, I called the therapist I'd used in the past. She

recommended going someplace safe. It was the first time in my life that thoughts of death had crept into my panic attacks. I was terrified. I

went to my parents' house because I was paranoid about being alone. They

weren't at home and I didn't want to call to alarm them... so I waited. I walked

down to their beach and lay in the sand, fully clothed. It was 75 degrees and I

was wearing a corduroy hat, black sweater, long jeans, black knee-length wool

jacket and cowboy boots. Without any towel, I flopped in the sand. I'm sure

boaters got an eyeful on their morning cruise.

I hadn't been on medication in two years. None. Pilots training doesn't

allow for any medication. With my history of severe anxiety and depression,

I thought that was progress. In fact I had forgotten that medication was

an option. I was used to pushing through (albeit mostly hysterical) and

trying to use breathing techniques as a calming force. The therapist had

reminded me to take an anxiety pill to try to relax. A pill? A pill. A pill! Yes,

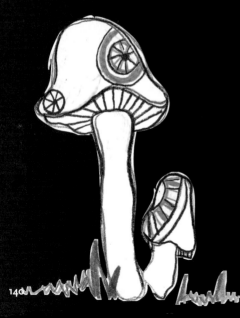

pills! Pills had escaped me as an option.

I was so relieved to have a pending way out.

My chest was full of fear. I couldn't see. The pill didn't work. I was still hyper-

ventilating. Thirty minutes later, I took another. I tried to keep the gathering snakes

in my mind from devouring me. Every twenty minutes I took another pill to keep my

chest from closing in. This was the scene my mother encountered in what became

the first day of a full-blown nervous breakdown.

I wound up in the emergency room, having Overdosed

and was admitted into our psychiatric hospital, Center One.

This was the explosion that changed my life. I was not only

brought to my knees; I was rendered childlike, unable to even shower. Having

experienced a "major depressive episode," I couldn't drive a car or do anything productive. My brain had completely short-circuited from overload.

A trip to the psych ward took me on a side trip, and down a scary alley I didn't see coming.

I spent three weeks as a patient in the hospital, one week in the center and two weeks in an outpatient facility. I lived for months in the darkest, most terrifying place of my mind; a hell I hope never to return to. Coming out of it has been gruelingly slow, and a full-time commitment to diet, drink, exercise, therapy, schedules, etc. Like a roller coaster, it has ups and downs. The downs are still terrifying as anyone with clinical depression knows. It is not like feeling sad. It is like feeling dead.

In the hospital I learned about brain function and what happens when a depression is left unattended. How in a clinical case, the brain actually begins to shut down. I saw images of a brain that looked like mine. Dark spots were manifesting on the frontal lobe. As part of our therapy, we were required to make one simple goal per day. The first two days, I managed to escape that commitment. The third day I was cornered. The nurse made a suggestion: "How about your goal for today is to take a shower?" That is how bad it was. My entire goal for the

day was to go to group meetings and make it through the showering process. Getting a towel

and shampoo together seemed overwhelming.

The patients in a depressive ward look like the living dead.

I had no will to live.

My parents, sister and ex-husband were called in to learn more about my illness.

They moved into my house and cared for me and my children. Months went by, and I

slowly started driving while trying to stabilize. My psychiatrist warned me it would be a

painstakingly slow process – and it was. She said I was so far below baseline it would

take several weeks to get my medication up to the required dose.

Nothing helped. I was still extremely depressed. I didn't feel better, even three months

later. We discussed other options, and in late January she showed concern that progress

was minimal.

she mentioned electro shock therapy

Shock therapy? Oh, my word... had it come to that? Were people really doing this? I was

frightened, but willing to try anything — *anything* to get out of the hell in which my brain

was residing. I prayed constantly. I still had art shows to do and work to manage. I forced

myself to do what was required, but my soul's light had gone out. I was an empty shell

and believed I would always be that way.

I felt horrible for my three children. They walked around with concerned looks and fretted

about my care. It was once again the "depressed Kristen" household, and I couldn't do

anything to normalize it. These kids had already seen me completely broken at the loss

of my marriage to their father. Here we were, four years later and back again. I forced

myself to stay awake and dragged myself out of bed to make a good show, but I couldn't

wait until everyone left for school so I could crawl back into bed.

Then grace was bestowed upon me.

One early morning in February I was sitting at the breakfast table listening to the radio and out of the blue, I heard myself laugh. It woke me up. I hadn't heard myself laugh in four months. I looked around suspiciously and realized that I felt OK. Like, as in good. Not even suicidal. I got up and paced around the table laughing and crying at the same time. The sun was beaming through the trees, right into my dining room and into my heart. I immediately began chanting out loud, "Thank you God, thank you God, thank you God!"

I scanned my brain, and the black cloud had lifted. The veil was gone. I felt like my old self. I called my mom.

That was the beginning. I am seeing light for the first time in years. It reveals a glow that is a fresh kind of alive. My life feels right. The good things are magnified into their full power, simply because the hideous black cloak is removed.

"There is no happiness in any place except what you bring to it yourself"

— Henry David Thoreau

At thirty-six, I have come to realize that as much as I've over-analyzed the workings of man and woman, I really don't know much of anything. Things that aren't supposed to work sometimes do. Others that were a sure thing, can flop. There are no guarantees. It's all a crazy journey.

We seem to suffer so, because we have gotten off track. At the end of the day, the big house, the fancy car, the beautiful body are all rendered meaningless when your soul is suffering. I have spent time at the "Acquire-More Mall," but now it's clear to me, my answers weren't there. If they aren't in the stuff, it makes sense that they aren't in the hard body either, or the mega job, or the marriage, or anything coming from the outside. Contentment resides in knowing I am fulfilling my universal commitment.

My rocket fuel is *contribution*; in giving rather than grasping. I've spent decades on a roller coaster, and I can promise you I pray everyday this little mantra:

"God, I want to be the person you would have me be. I want to see with your eyes, hear with your ears, speak with your tongue and love with your heart. I am open to you. I want to help you heal the world. I will do whatever it takes. Please use me."

And I mean it.

And my life has completely transformed.

As the world turns on its axis and plays out my drama, I pray that my work will contribute

something real, meaningful and healing to the world. I want to be a part of the solution.

I hope to eventually break free of my neuroses and the many things that get in my way

and then smile – knowing that in some small way I made a positive difference.

So, when I get knocked down by facing the demons of my past, or even sabotage myself

with the fear of success, I will struggle to get back up. I will try again. I might cry. I might

be a real bitch for a few days. I might get sick again (God help me). I might crawl into a

hole and have to be drawn out, but I will get up. I will eventually get right with myself. I

will move forward toward the light and toward love.

"It takes 43 muscles to frown and only 17 to smile, but it doesn't take any to just sit there with a dumb look on your face."

- Anonymous

Ho Ho Ho

a Holiday Newsletter from the Jongens

and Greetings of the Season to family and friends!

The Jongens are proud to announce our first Christmas newsletter! In an effort to keep up with the Joneses, we thought we'd do a little boasting, ourselves.

This has been a banner year for us, with so many things to brag about. Ahh, where to begin?

For starters, our neighborhood Association reversed its previous decision and decided to let us stay (it only required a small fee). Although we're not allowed to participate in communal activities, we can watch from a distance! We had great seats for the Bar-B-Q... it was a blast!

Our new little prince, Van Michael, finally grew tired of waiting and learned to change his own diaper! The doctors say he is genius material. Though not a demonstrative boy, Van uses sign language proficiently.

His favorite gesture is to give his sisters the middle finger. All this and he's only two! Can you imagine?

Of course we think it's adorable.

Mia turned nine this year. After a few minor setbacks, she is finally ready for Kindergarten next fall. We knew she could do it! Mia cannot wait to start socializing with other kids. A bit on the eccentric side, she likes to collect garbage and fruit pits.

Anya is becoming quite a looker. An official teenager now, she loves doing teen things (deer hunting and four wheeling top the charts). Hormones continue to rage, but we have a dart gun lovingly referred to as "the family therapist." If she gets out of control, we're all proficient in administering a quick shot to the neck. Works like a charm.

Kristen has developed a brisk business with funeral parlors. Her poetry has truly found its

niche there. When not working or creating her "idiosyncratic" art, she's been learning to drive a

snowplow – which is great for winter fun. The neighbors refer to her as "one of the guys."

Finances are better than ever. We just rotated the wheels on the house and pulled into our winter

spot. We'll be nailing lattice around the bottom this weekend and rolling out the deck! With our

bonus (an undisclosed sum) we've invested wisely – changing the color of the door knobs and

laying down fresh Astroturf.

Curious updates:

The department of Social Services ruled that with a little housecleaning, Kristen will be allowed to keep the kids.

The lice situation worked itself out.

Mom's nose piercing eventually healed.

The truancy police have finally backed off (perhaps because of frustration).

Mia's shark teeth are under surveillance; contrary to opinion humans really can grow teeth in multiple rows.

In conjunction with other family matters, tests reveal that Anya is not deaf. She simply has a bad attitude.

Van is neither deaf nor blind. He just doesn't watch or listen.

Kristen is looking seriously into investing in a dollar-ama.

Umm, regarding the embarrassing scene at the bar. Although still

unwilling to marry Kristen, the eye doctor decided to drop the

charges. A strange fellow, he accused her of being a man. He has

not changed his mind, however.

Perhaps this little dose of heaven

will inspire you to come for a visit?

Happy Holidays and Blessings, one and all!

We hope our good fortune spills in your direction.

P.S. After you read this, and if you wouldn't mind sending it on to the names listed below, it would really help us out with postage costs.

P.P.S. If you want to support the children (they all need new underpants), check out our website for information on the Jongen charity at www.mysoulsoup.com. Credit cards are joyfully accepted.

full rich

It has been almost a year since my nervous breakdown. It is a very dark time to remember and a place where I am terrified to return. Now I am running again on four cylinders, even though one or more may misfire at any given time.

Everything has changed since lift-off from that fearful space. Looking back, I have learned something critical about living my life full-throttle: racing full-speed burns a lot of gas.

I'd been chasing down my life, terrified it might slip through my grasp. I lived the phrase, "If this can happen, *anything* can happen," in response to major setbacks. More frequently I reminded myself I could die tomorrow. There is no universal safety net. There is no quota for tragedies. Bad things can happen to good people at any time, and riding into a carefree sunset is an illusion.

So, the solution appeared to be this;

devour life
without stopping to chew

Consume experiences and opportunities rabidly – lest they slip away. Move ahead with ferocious

speed, so the past couldn't catch up and shackle me.

A year of retrospect has been good. Looking back has its place in recovery.

As Debussy said, "Music is the space between the notes"

the silence between words makes the poem

and the seemingly-disastrous in-between spots in life bear the miracles. I've learned that when I begin to

fret about my work, my boyfriend, my kids, my parents and my future... I lose sight of myself. Where did

Kristen go? Where is her soul? Are they together?

I mentally unhinge my clinging self from the subject of my panic and come to stillness. This has been

my greatest lesson.

It is the conscious and constant shifting back toward my center that is my saving grace. It points me away from the chaos in my head and has me staring into the God that lives within me. I am stunned at how many times I have to travel around the moon just to land exactly where I launched my journey. The road always leads me home; to me, my Spirit and my God.

I am no longer interested in living life full throttle; the wear and tear on my nerves is too much. Instead I have traded one flight training term for another. I have traded full throttle for full rich. I don't want to cast wider.

I want to burn deeper.

Full rich is in flying terms the richest mixture of oil and gasoline. I want to enrich the experiences I have now, with my children, my family, my friends and my life's work. I want to live with purpose instead of panic. I want to continue to write about things that matter. This means I need to be fully present, especially in the little things.

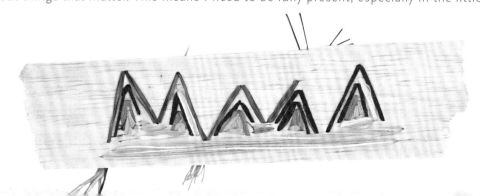

I have been so lost, that it feels wonderful to find myself again. My answers come to me in the simplest forms of joy, like my son's first missing tooth. I am relishing this time alone, sans a love affair to complicate things. Actually loving it. Focusing on my kids and work is enough. Our crew is no longer in missing-man formation; we are the Jongens as an adjoining whole. We feel free to discover "us" in different ways now. We have a new scent, energy and certainly a rowdier sense of humor. *I mean, if you can't laugh at a trip to the loony bin, what can you laugh at?* I love who we have grown to be, and am grateful that I get to be the mom. I am proud of who we are.

I will continue to let my wings dry and practice aeronautical maneuvers in between. I will flop and fail and make a spectacle of myself as usual. I haven't changed *that* much!

I will no longer ask for Peace as if it is a hopeless Request that answers back. I have it in my Pocket, and it is Leaking Out. I am Leaking Out. bestowed by some third party. I will reclaim Ownership because It is rightfully Mine. I will practice what I preach I am willing to be peace with you my mama taught me to share. and feed it with a net that Listens, and a Love

160

© 2010 Soul Soup

I want to soar with the best and be just as content on the ground. Some days flying looks a lot less like "Out of Africa" and more like watching "The Dog Whisperer" with my kids.

As I finish up the final chapter of this book, it is 3:19 am. I am lying on my couch, using a pile of clean laundry as a pillow. I will drive Mia to her doctor appointment in Grand Rapids (2.5 hours away) tomorrow, err... today. On our porch steps I can see the glowing candles from the pumpkins we carved last night. It is still two full weeks to Halloween.

I have to smile at our similarities with those annoying people from the farmers' market a few years ago. Maybe I will surprise the kids and make them fresh organic star fruit smoothies for breakfast?

Ha! Maybe not. I haven't changed *that* much!

I have learned that my life right here in my small town is exactly the life I am supposed to be living. My "real" life is not happening in Hawaii with a surfer... It is not waiting for me in New York, either. I am where my life is, and beautiful things happen everywhere. God breathes in every corner of the Universe. Even in tiny places like Traverse City, Michigan. I believe we are all born with 100% of God's light. Nothing else matters except love. Our mission on earth is to heal each other, the planet, and the entire kingdom. Everything derives from that urge to heal. The void we feel is the abyss we feed with things, *items*. I think inherently we know that our lives hold greater purpose. We are born to contribute to the solution. We have a responsibility to share the garden with everyone and make sure everyone is fed. Everyone. If we constantly reach toward love, how can we go wrong?

The suit of wings is pretty cool. It's getting comfy. I always knew I was a butterfly; I was only confused on the type.

I didn't realize my colors would shine the brightest against the Midwestern sun in my own front yard.

My sweetheart said to me at dinner when we first started dating, "You are very difficult to get to know." I was aghast! Me? Ms. Poet of my Life? Ms. Spills her Guts on canvas for everyone to see?

"Yes, you, Kristen Lynne," he said with a smirk.

"You surprise me all the time," He continued.

Pause.

There was a time in my life where the exact opposite was true. I couldn't wait to push myself down someone's throat. There was never enough space to "discover" anything. An introduction revealed my favorite food, first words and natural hair color within three minutes.

I *have* changed.

Funny how this lesson comes full circle for me and Soul Soup... and all the resources I have spent in packaging both. My little company has never been jump-started by press and accolades.

because
Love is still bigger

My words do best when they are not thrust upon someone, but when they are discovered.

The quiet underground of people who find me, uncover my work and pass it on to one another has procured my success. So as I finish this book, I pray once again that we will find each other. That in these pages, there is a glimmer of truth that speaks to others.

With nothing left to prove, I release the reins and trust that life is headed where it is supposed to go. Little chapters add up to complete volumes – but for now it is perfectly OK to close one small book. I feel content soaring into flight when inspired. I am also learning to trust that there is a different kind of serenity in moments gathered only on the ground – both can create a sense of peace that allows me to feel content, safe, and simply...

happy.

grow
grow
grow

big

akeru:

To begin, to end, to empty, to open, to dawn,

to unlock, to become daylight, to grow light,

to make a hole, to unwrap, to clearout,

to make space for.